Doggie Tails with Alex and Andria In Alexandria

Written and Illustrated by

Patricia McMullin Palermino

Tattle Tale Publishing

PUBLISHED BY TATTLE TALE PUBLISHING
AND PATRICIA PALERMINO STUDIO, LLC

FIRST EDITION

LIBRARY OF CONGRESS CATALOGING - IN - PUBLICATION DATA
PALERMINO, PATRICIA.
DOGGIE TAILS OF ALEX AND ANDRIA IN ALEXANDRIA/
PATRICIA PALERMINO P. CM.
SUMMARY : TWO SCOTTISH TERRIERS TAKE THE READER ON A TOUR OF
ALEXANDRIA FROM THE PERSPECTIVE OF A DOG.....
1. ALEXANDRIA-FICTION.
2. DOGS-FICTION.
3. SCOTTISH TERRIERS-FICTION.
1. PALERMINO, PATRICIA, ILL. 11. TITLE
ISBN 978-0-9788627-0-1
ISBN 0-9788627-0-8

THE ILLUSTRATIONS IN THIS BOOK WERE PAINTED IN ACRYLICS ON CANVAS.
TYPE AND GRAPHIC DESIGN BY JANE ANDRLE GILETTE

Printed and bound in China

THIS BOOK IS DEDICATED TO MY WONDERFUL FAMILY: JERRY, BETH, JAY, LISA AND MY SPECIAL GRANDBOYS, EVAN, CAMERON, ETHAN AND MAX. THE GRANDBOYS HAVE KEPT US YOUNG AT HEART AND SHOWN US HOW TO LOVE LIFE LIKE A CHILD AGAIN.

I CANNOT FORGET OUR CANINE PALS, PHOEBE AND WINSTON, WHO HELPED ME TO SEE THE WORLD FROM THE STREET LEVEL.

ONCE UPON A TIME THERE WERE TWO LITTLE SCOTTY DOGS, ALEX AND ANDRIA, WHO WERE BROTHER AND SISTER.

EVERYONE THINKS THAT THEY WERE NAMED FOR THE CITY OF ALEXANDRIA WHERE THEY LIVE.

ALEX AND ANDRIA LIVE ON THE TOP FLOOR OF POPS WONDERFUL ICE CREAM STORE. THEY LOVE LIVING ON TOP OF POPS BECAUSE THEY LOVE ICE CREAM CONES AND THEY LOVE LIVING IN ALEXANDRIA BECAUSE THERE ARE SO MANY FUN THINGS TO DO AND ALEXANDRIA LOVES DOGGIES!

ONE OF THEIR MOST FAVORITE PLACES TO GO IS TO THE FARMER'S MARKET AT MARKET SQUARE ON SATURDAY MORNINGS. THEY SEE ALL OF THEIR FRIENDS FROM DOGGIE SCHOOL AND SMILE AT THE FARMERS WHO GIVE THEM LOTS OF TREATS.

SOMETIMES THEY ARE VERY NAUGHTY AND PUSH EACH OTHER INTO THE BIG POOL WITH THE FOUNTAIN. DOGGIES ARE NOT ALLOWED TO SWIM IN THE POOL! ANDRIA ALWAYS WEARS GOGGLES BECAUSE SHE THINKS NO ONE WILL RECOGNIZE HER! THEY ARE ALWAYS CAUGHT, BUT IT IS SO MUCH FUN!!

ALEX AND ANDRIA GO WINDOW SHOPPING ON KING STREET AND PEEK IN THE RESTAURANTS THAT ALWAYS SMELL SO GOOD. mmmmmmm!

ALEX TRIES ON NEW CLOTHES IN THEIR FAVORITE SCOTTY STORE. HE IS GETTING READY FOR ALL OF THE PARTIES AND PARADES TO BE HELD IN HIS HONOR AS THE MASCOT OF THE ALEXANDRIA CONVENTION AND VISITORS CENTER AT THE RAMSAY HOUSE. ANDRIA WATCHES AND TELLS HIM HOW HANDSOME HE LOOKS. SHE LOVES HER BIG BROTHER!

CAN YOU GUESS WHERE THEY GO ON TUESDAY AND THURSDAY?

DOGGIE HAPPY HOUR!!

THEY MEET THEIR DOGGIE PALS IN THE COURTYARD ON KING STREET AND SNACK ON DOGGIE COOKIES AND DRINKS FROM THEIR VERY OWN DOGGIE DISHES.

YOU CAN EVEN HAVE YOUR PHOTO TAKEN WITH ALEX AND HIS FRIENDS!

DOGGIE HAPPY HOUR
COOKIES ★ SNACKS ★ DRINKS
PHOTOS WITH ALEX AND ANDRIA
BEAR
FRED
DOLLY
ALEX
COOKIES
RILEY
MUFFIN
FLUFFY

ALL YEAR LONG THERE ARE PARADES IN ALEXANDRIA TO CELEBRATE SPECIAL DAYS. A VERY SPECIAL DAY IS GEORGE WASHINGTON'S BIRTHDAY WHEN THE FIFE AND DRUMS BANDS PLAY. GEORGE WASHINGTON WAS OUR FIRST PRESIDENT AND HE WENT TO GADSBY'S TAVERN FROM MOUNT VERNON FOR PARTIES AND BALLS IN HIS HONOR!

ALEX AND ANDRIA RIDE IN A CARRIAGE IN THE PARADE AND SMILE BIG SMILES AND WAVE THEIR PAWS. THEY FEEL SOOO GRAND!

ALEXANDRIA HAS A DOGGIE SHOW ON SAINT PATRICK'S DAY AT MARKET SQUARE. IT TAKES PLACE AFTER THE EXCITING SAINT PATRICK'S DAY PARADE. DOGGIES CAME FROM NEAR AND FAR TO TRY TO WIN BLUE RIBBONS.

ANDRIA WINS THE 'CUTEST' DOG RIBBON AND ALEX IS THE 'MOST SCOTTISH'!! THE POODLE IS THE 'PUFFIEST' AND THE WESTIE IS THE 'WHITEST'.

THE POTOMAC RIVER BOAT COMPANY HAS SPECIAL "CANINE CRUISES" TO TAKE ALEX AND ANDRIA AND THEIR FRIENDS UP AND DOWN THE POTOMAC RIVER. IT'S FUN TO BARK AT THE DUCKS AND TO HEAR ALL ABOUT MOUNT VERNON.

OLD TOWN HAS A PARK JUST FOR DOGGIES TO RUN AND PLAY. ALEX PLAYS 'CATCH' AND ANDRIA GOES SNORKELING.

WHEN SUMMER COMES AND DOGGIE SCHOOL IS OVER, ALEX AND ANDRIA CAN HARDLY WAIT FOR THE WATERFRONT FESTIVAL. THERE ARE SCARY RIDES, COTTON CANDY, MUSIC, FIREWORKS AND VERY TALL SHIPS.

THEY LOVE THE FERRIS WHEEL THE BEST. THEY LAUGH AND SCREAM WHEN THE BIG WHEEL ROCKS THEM BACK AND FORTH!

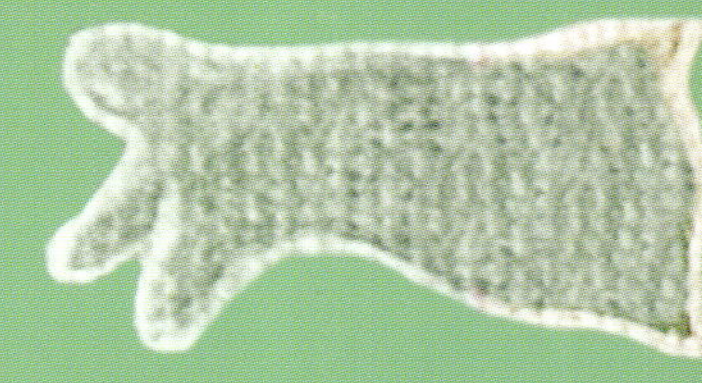

ALEX AND ANDRIA LOVE TO GO ON THE "GHOST TOURS" WITH THE LADY DRESSED IN COLONIAL COSTUME. IT IS SOOO SPOOKY!

IF YOU LOOK HARD ENOUGH YOU CAN SEE THE GHOSTS FOLLOWING ALONG !

ON HALLOWEEN ALEX AND ANDRIA DRESS UP IN THEIR COSTUMES AND MARCH IN THE "HALLOWEEN DOGGIE PARADE". A WITCH DIRECTS TRAFFIC ON KING STREET AND GHOSTS FLOAT AROUND. ALEX IS "SNEEZY", ONE OF THE SEVEN DWARFS.

ANDRIA IS A BUMBLE BEE. THEY MAKE AH-CHOOO AND BZZZZZZ SOUNDS AND EVERYONE LAUGHS!

THE PARADE ALEX AND ANDRIA LOVE THE BEST IS THE SCOTTISH WALK. EVERYBODY WEARS PLAID KILTS AND HATS TO CELEBRATE ALEXANDRIA'S SCOTTISH HERITAGE. ALEX LEADS THE PARADE WITH HIS BIG BATON.

ANDRIA MARCHES WITH THE "SCOTTY + FRIENDS BRIGADE". THE BAGPIPES PLAY AND IT IS SUCH A FUN DAY!

WHEN IT IS ALMOST CHRISTMAS, ALEX AND ANDRIA GO TO VISIT SANTA CLAUS. THEY STAND IN LINE WITH ALL THE DOGGIES OF ALEXANDRIA TO TELL SANTA THAT THEY HAVE BEEN VERY GOOD DOGGIES.

ANDRIA SNEAKS AWAY TO HAVE SANTA COOKIES AND YUMMY EGGNOG IN THE DOGGIE BAKERY. SANTA TELLS ANDRIA IF SHE ISN'T A GOOD DOOGIE SHE WILL NOT HAVE A STOCKING FILLED WITH GOODIES ON CHRISTMAS DAY! THAT ANDRIA IS SUCH A RASCAL!

A BIG CHRISTMAS TREE IS LIT AT MARKET SQUARE IN DECEMBER.

EVERYONE COMES TO WATCH AND TO SING CHRISTMAS CAROLS. THE CITY IF FILLED WITH GOOD CHEER!

P.Palermino ©

ALEX AND ANDRIA WATCH THE LIGHTING OF THE CHRISTMAS TREE TOO. THEY SING CAROLS AND HAVE LOTS OF COOKIES WITH THEIR FRIENDS AND WISH EVERYONE "MERRY CHRISTMAS"!

IT IS A MAGICAL NIGHT !
ALEX AND ANDRIA LOVE ALEXANDRIA!

WHAT DO YOU THINK ??

A LITTLE QUIZ FOR LITTLE PEOPLE WHO LOVE LITTLE DOGGIES LIKE ALEX AND ANDRIA

1. DO YOU THINK THAT ALEX AND ANDRIA WERE REALLY NAMED FOR THE CITY OF ALEXANDRIA?

2. DO DOGGIES REALLY WEAR GOGGLES? DO THEY GO SNORKELING?

3. HAVE YOU EVER SEEN DOGGIES SWIMMING IN THE FOUNTAIN AT MARKET SQUARE?

4. IS THERE REALLY A SCOTTY STORE IN ALEXANDRIA?

5. HAVE YOU AND YOUR MOM OR DAD EVER GONE TO SEE THE DOGGIES AT "DOGGIE HAPPY HOUR"?

6. DO DOGGIES RIDE IN CARRIAGES WITH PONIES?

7. DO YOU THINK THAT DOGGIES REALLY GO ON "CANINE CRUISES"?

8. DO YOU THINK THERE ARE REALLY GHOSTS IN ALEXANDRIA? HAVE YOU EVER SEEN A DOGGIE GHOST?

9. DOES ALEX REALLY LEAD THE SCOTTISH WALK PARADE?

I HOPE THAT YOU HAD A FUN TIME READING ABOUT MY FAVORITE DOGGIES IN THE WHOLE, WIDE WORLD!!!

PATRICIA PALERMINO